Code R...

by Jo Cott...
Illustrated by ...

OXFORD

UNIVERSITY PRESS

In this story ...

Cam
(Switch)

Cam has the power to turn into animals. She is most proud of the time she stopped some baddies from robbing a bank by turning into a giraffe.

Axel
(Invisiboy)

Pip
(Boost)

Nisha
(Nimbus)

Slink
(Combat Cat)

Chapter 1:
HATs

"I can't do it," Axel said, thumping his book down on the bench. "I just can't remember all this stuff. It's too hard."

"I know tests are scary," Cam told him, "but you're not going to fail. I know you can do it."

The two friends were sitting in the gardens of Hero Academy. They were studying for the Hero Academy Tests, or HATs, the most important tests of the year.

"When I'm feeling worried," Cam said, "I close my eyes and breathe very slowly. Then I count to ten. When I open my eyes, I feel much better."

Axel nodded. "I'll try to remember that."

"You just need to relax," Cam added.

"You're right," said Axel, picking up his bag. "I think I'll go and play a game of Powerball. Are you coming?"

"Maybe later," Cam replied.

As Axel walked away, Cam saw Mr Trainer coming along the path towards her.

"Good work, Cam," said Mr Trainer. "I overheard you talking. You showed great hero qualities there."

Cam got to her feet. "I wasn't even using my powers!"

"Yes you were. Superpowers aren't always things like invisibility or flying." Mr Trainer smiled. "By the way, the Head would like to see you."

"Does he have a mission for me?" Cam asked, excitedly.

"Why don't you go and find out?" replied Mr Trainer.

Chapter 2:
The new mission

Cam knocked on the Head's door and entered. She was surprised to see Slink sitting in the chair by the Head's desk.

"Hello, Slink!" said Cam. "I thought you were out looking for new superheroes to join the academy."

"He's just got back," the Head said, appearing from the holo-projector on his desk. "In fact, that's why I sent for you."

Slink

Catchphrase: Meow!

Hobbies: sleeping, eating.

Likes: Scrummy-Yums cat food, being stroked just behind his right ear.

Dislikes: being woken up suddenly, running out of Scrummy-Yums.

Slink is no ordinary cat. He finds children with superpowers and then reports back to the Head. When he has found a new hero, the red lights on his collar turn green.

Slink can turn into **Combat Cat** and is a martial arts expert.

"I have a new mission for you," the Head continued, "but it could be very difficult."

Cam stood up straight. "I can do it," she replied confidently.

"Slink has found a potential pupil," the Head said. "A boy with strong powers. We want him to come to Hero Academy."

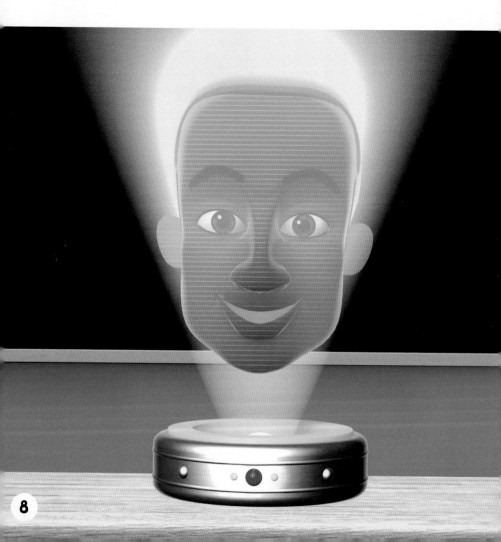

An image appeared on the screen behind the Head. It showed a boy with brown hair, standing in the middle of a bedroom. He looked very unhappy.

"This is Neo," said the Head. "He has water powers, but he can't control them yet. He used to go to Superpower School ..." The Head's voice grew sharper as he named the rival school. "He ran away and went back home, and now Neo says he'll never go to school again. I've offered him a place here, but he won't come."

"Poor Neo," said Cam, looking at the picture of the miserable boy. "What do you want me to do?"

The Head smiled at her. "This mission needs someone with special powers."

"Shape-shifting?" asked Cam.

"No, not shape-shifting," said the Head. "What Neo needs more than anything is a friend. You're a good listener. I'd like you to persuade Neo to come to Hero Academy. Slink will show you where he lives."

Slink jumped down from the chair and rubbed up against Cam's legs, purring.

"I'll do my very best, sir," said Cam.

Chapter 3:
Neo

Later that day, Cam and Slink set off, leaving the academy through the secret door and entering an ordinary street. From the outside, no one would guess that there was an entire school behind Door 62!

Cam became Switch and shape-shifted into a cat, so she and Slink were able to cross rooftops and fences together. Soon, they reached Neo's flat, which was on the edge of Lexis City.

Cam changed back into her human form and rang the doorbell while Slink settled down next to a pot plant in the hall for a quick catnap.

The door opened, and Neo stood in front of Cam. "Hello?" he said, in an uncertain voice.

Cam smiled. "Hi. I'm Cam, from Hero Academy. May I come in?"

Neo frowned. "I already told them, I'm not going. You can't make me!" He started to close the door.

"Wait!" said Cam. "Please. I didn't come here to make you do anything. I came because I thought you might need a friend."

Neo hesitated. "A friend?" he said.

"Who's at the door?" called a man, from further inside the flat.

"It's a girl from the other school," Neo called back. He turned to Cam. "You'd better come in, but we'll need to be quiet. Dad does shift work at the dam. He sometimes sleeps during the day."

Cam followed Neo into the flat. "Are you sure you won't think about coming to the academy?" she asked. "You'd have lots of friends."

"I'm not going!" Neo said through gritted teeth. As he spoke, water sprayed out of his hands and soaked the floor in front of them. "Now look what you made me do!"

"I'm sorry," said Cam. "I didn't mean to upset you."

"No, I'm sorry." Neo looked away. "I've never been very good at controlling my powers," he said in a muffled voice. "The kids at my last school used to laugh at me."

"How horrible of them," said Cam. "But my friends aren't like that. There's Pip: she's super strong and super helpful. Nisha can control the weather, and she's really funny. Axel can turn invisible. He's really kind and a bit shy …"

Cam told Neo all about life at Hero Academy and all about her friends. As she talked, Cam noticed that the water from the drenched floor began to lift up in tiny droplets. The droplets drifted back towards Neo in a line. He turned his hands upwards, sending them spinning in a spiral above his head.

"That's beautiful," said Cam, looking at the watery spiral.

Neo looked at his hands in surprise.

The water droplets fell from the air and splattered on to the carpet.

"See?" he said bitterly. "I can only do it if I'm not thinking about it. I'm a failure."

A mobile phone rang suddenly, making them both jump. Cam heard Neo's dad's voice from the other room. Then the bedroom door was flung open and Neo's dad rushed out, reaching for his high-vis vest.

"I have to go," he said.

"What's happened, Dad?" asked Neo.

"Can't stop," said his dad. "It's a Code Red!"

Neo's dad threw on his high-vis vest and ran out of the front door.

Neo and Cam hurried to the window. A minute later, they heard a car start up and saw Neo's dad drive away.

Chapter 4:
Everyone is in danger!

"What's a Code Red?" asked Cam.

Neo turned to her, a frightened look in his eyes. "It means the dam is failing."

"Failing?" asked Cam. "You mean it could burst?"

Neo nodded.

Cam took a deep breath. "But, if the dam breaks, all that water will come flooding into Lexis City. Everyone is in danger! Neo, we have to help!"

"*We*?" Neo said. "I can't do anything."

Cam faced Neo. "You can control water! Come with me to the dam."

"No," said Neo, shaking his head. "I won't be any use. I'll only make things worse."

"You don't know that! Please, Neo!" pleaded Cam. "My shape-shifting powers alone won't be enough to stop a flood. I can't do this by myself. I need your help."

Neo hesitated. "We won't get there in time."

"Yes, we will." Cam threw open the front door. "Slink!" she yelled. "Call for back-up! The dam is failing! Follow me, Neo." She raced down the stairs and out into the street, spinning into her super suit. There, Switch took a deep breath, focused and changed into a horse.

"Wow!" exclaimed Neo. "That's amazing!"

The horse whinnied and twitched her head. Gingerly, Neo climbed up and held on tightly to her mane. Switch took off, galloping through the streets, past astonished pedestrians and drivers.

Lexis City Dam

The Lexis City Dam helps control the flow of water from the river. It stops Lexis City from flooding. There is a reservoir – a large pool of water – behind the dam, which provides drinking water for the city.

Chapter 5:
Cracks!

As they neared the dam, Switch and Neo could hear sirens and alarms wailing. A large crack had appeared in the huge wall, and smaller cracks were spreading out from it.

Neo slid off Switch's back. She trotted behind a big truck and transformed back into a human.

Neo and Cam stared up at the wall, which was creaking ominously. There were distant shouts from the workers at the dam, and a trickle of water ran down the wall.

"It's going to give way!" someone yelled from the top of the dam. "Evacuate!"

Neo stepped back in shock. "That's my dad's voice! He's up there!"

People started running away from the dam.

"Neo," Cam said. "You have to hold back the water until the other heroes arrive."

Neo shook his head. "I ... I can't!"

Cam remembered what she had said to Axel earlier that day. "Close your eyes," she told Neo. "Breathe. Count to ten really slowly. It's just like the water you were controlling earlier. Trust yourself."

Neo closed his eyes and stretched out his hands towards the wall. "One ... two ... three ..." he began to count.

The trickle of water lifted off the wall. Droplets drifted through the air. Then they began to rise, back up to the cracks.

The wall groaned ... and then a whole section of the dam broke away, sending concrete slabs crashing to the ground.

Cam flinched, expecting the water to come flooding out, but it stayed where it was, as if being held by an invisible wall.

"You're doing it!" she whispered to Neo. "You're holding it back!"

Sweat broke out on Neo's forehead.
His arms began to tremble. "There's so
much of it!" he panted. "So … heavy!"

Cam knew Neo couldn't hold it for long. What could she do? Desperately, she looked around. Then she saw Nisha, in her Nimbus super suit, running towards them.

"Keep going!" Nimbus yelled at Neo. "You're doing brilliantly!" She stopped next to him and reached her arms up too. Instantly, clouds started to gather over the dam, and the temperature fell rapidly. "I can freeze it!" she said.

"Coming through!" shouted a voice. Pip, in her Boost super suit, raced to the break in the dam. She started lifting the heavy stones, piling them up against the dam to strengthen it.

Meanwhile, ice crystals spread across the water, hardening it into a solid wall.

Neo's arms finally gave way and he collapsed to the ground!

"You did it, Neo!" Cam cried. "I knew you could!" She heard footsteps behind her. She looked round but couldn't see anyone. Then Axel, dressed as Invisiboy, appeared next to her.

"What can I do?" he asked.

Cam suggested that Invisiboy go and switch all the alarms off so the engineers would know that it was safe to come back.

Just then, Neo's dad came running down the
steps of the dam towards them. "Neo! You're a
hero!" he said.

"Me?" said Neo.

"Of course!" Cam replied. "Now, come and meet
my friends."

Everyone shook Neo's hand, and his dad led a round of cheering.

Neo felt so proud he lifted a hand into the air and sent a jet of water up like a fountain. It sprinkled tiny rainbow droplets on to everyone below.

"Awesome work, Neo," said Invisiboy. "Is it true you're coming to our school?"

Neo looked at his dad. Then he looked at Cam, who was smiling. "Yes," he said, taking a deep breath. "Yes, I am."